Our Neighborhood

Piper Nelid

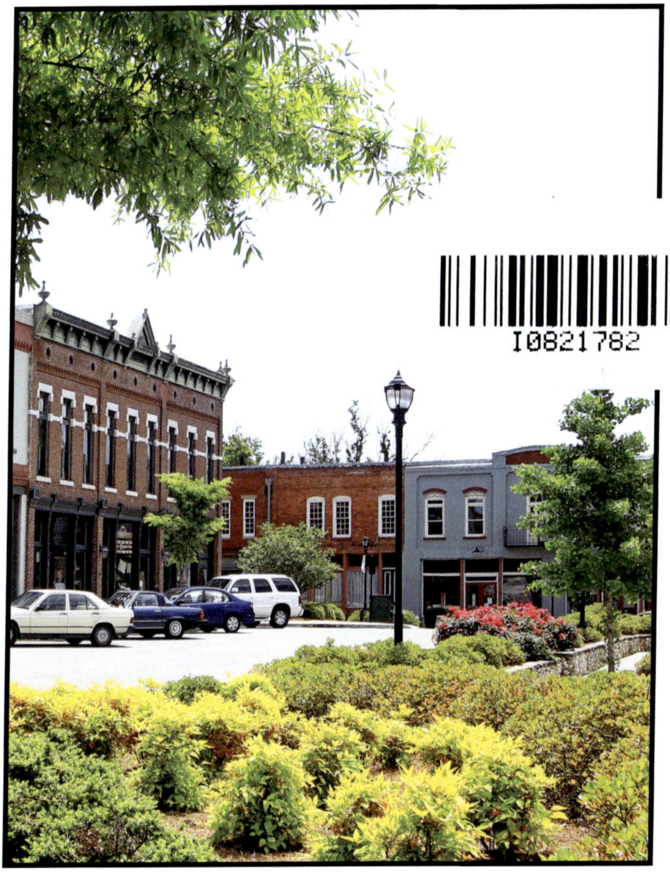

This is our neighborhood.

I meet my friends
in our neighborhood.

We walk to the library
to get books.

We go to the mall to shop.

We go to the park to play.

We go to the diner to eat lunch.

Words To Know

diner

friends

library

mall